I0756299

FINISHING LINE PRESS
www.finishinglinepress.com

Lucky to Have You

poems by

Dr. Sarah Jefferis

Finishing Line Press
Georgetown, Kentucky

Lucky to Have You

ISBN 979-8-89990-482-0 First Edition

Publisher: Leah Huete de Maines
Editor: Christen Kincaid
Cover Art: Charisse Green
Author Photo: Holly Green
Cover Design: Diane Cuddy

Order online: www.finishinglinepress.com
also available on amazon.com

Author inquiries and mail orders:
Finishing Line Press
PO Box 1626
Georgetown, Kentucky 40324
USA

Contents

All the love for my children—Ilah and Frida, whom, without their patience and faith in me as the poet mama goose, I wouldn't have the courage to rise and write.

The Assistant

In the dream, I am in the box, and you saw me in half.
My red heels stick outside of this coffin.

My top half rolls around the magician
and I smile and wave at the women in the audience.

They wave back.
Cheer me on.

Tell me to keep pressing
forward. Then I am the top-hatted

magician sawing myself
in half in a drawer,

as if I have been doing this my whole life
and calling it love,

and then I am in the audience
seeing myself halve myself

in this coffin; how is that I can be in half
and whole. Or somehow, in all three bodies,

and why does the metal of the saw
go back and forth like a metronome.

You always cut on the pull.
And what tempo could possibly stitch me back together again?

I. Lucky to Find You

Everyone in me is a bird.
I am beating all my wings.
They wanted to cut you out
But they will not.
They said you were immeasurably empty
But you are not.
They said you were sick unto dying.
But they were wrong.
You are singing like a schoolgirl.

Anne Sexton

The Lime Green Chairs

I come from the waters, soaking the green kneelers and the blood my mama turned her head away from that morning and all the mornings before and the mornings after. I come from the egg floating inside my mama who was inside her mama who heard voices. I come from the grandmama whose voices told her to basket her child for the nuns on cathedral steps in Philly and walk away in 1939. I come from nine beads and Latin, from graves beneath the stone floor, from wax dripping on my mama's hand, from the half note in the hymnal, from the "Lord Have Mercy" in *The Book of Common Prayer,* from wide box pews which for centuries creased in colonizers. I come from the priest who left the liturgy and waddled with her to the hospital. I come from the orange Pinto, she folded herself in, from the polyester seat she soaked through. I come from the lime green chairs she slipped on, the silver ticking clock in the lobby, and the unexpected snowflakes in Virginia. I come from the woman who said: *Ma'am, not here, we have a room, Ma'am, well then.* I come from the star-singing boatman rocking his sail, too far in the Atlantic to turn back before my first breath.

What Father Michael Gave Me In Virginia

I.
votive candles, a bowl to wash my feet,
twenties, my first driving lesson

a sea monster   seagulls from the James
Olive Garden leftovers

a caged bird   the Psalms
a pickle bin, a checking account

a concussion from a tent pole
Vacation Bible School "The Love Shack"

an obtrusive sandbar   rug burn
Oscar Romero   The AIDS Quilt

turquoise bracelets   cheese sandwiches
Emily Dickinson   Montblancs

rags to wipe kneelers   oxen at the gate
Victoria's Secret panties   tickets to Missoula Montana

red clay   tabletop gravestones
a high pulpit with a sounding board

my first sermon   the Gnostic Gospels
John D. Rockefeller   Cotesworth Lewis

The oldest hospital in Virginia   peach lipstick
the Tarpley Bell from 1761   Days Inn keys

The Book of Common Prayer   gas money
a canopy over The Governor's Pew   Stockholm

Let me not to the marriage of true minds admit impediments
Love is not love which alters when it alteration finds

James Blair William Archer Rutherford Goodwin
President Roosevelt's bronze lectern

Angel's right foot in the Old World with the British lion
The left foot in the New World near the Americas

King Edward's Bible
Denny's All-You-Can-Eat   my first job in a nursery

Lay your sleeping head, my love
Human on my faithless arm

a set of pans   college tuition
horse shit and drumsticks   the Jamestown Baptismal font

Time and fevers burn away
Individual beauty from

heels to click on the dead
boxes of vegetable lo mein

keys to trespassing myself
a prescription to all the blue pills

I could swallow

II.

In how many tongues was I taught to say help yourself
How many times have I closed my eyes
to not watch all the ways he has
And if I had kept them open, could I have stopped him
How many altars have I laid my legs upon
How many hours have I begged for deliverance
How many tongues was I taught to say help yourself
How many tongues was I taught
How many tongues was I
How many tongues
How many
How

Walking to Bruton Parish Church

A broken seesaw behind a gas station laundromat
looks like a babysitter.

The burgundy Pinto on cinder blocks
a home for fruit flies

who sing over Chef Boyardee in black bags on the curb.
My blind, heavy mama begs Jesus for quarters.

Down the way past the oxen knocking on gates,
the snap of paddocks

and the costumed and wigged
pretend to be British.

The stink of horseshit on the pebble road.
The fife and drum marching through piles.

All this before your kiss
in the closet behind an altar

as you straightened your collar, shook incense,
while the organ moaned for your appearance.

The sacristy was a coffin, for me,
and all creatures, great and small.

My Mama's Second Husband

Whoever lost the most weight in a month
        got McDonald's fries and a gospel album.
                We were not allowed to play gospel

when Mama's husband was home.
        He didn't love the Son the way we did.
                Didn't believe in rapture.

His own belly pinned
        in the cockpit of a Pinto.
                Not quite the coffin from the payment plan.

Jaws of Death called to unhinge him.
        On the empty fridge we had a sticker chart
                with smiley faces.

I staggered, which fingers I slid past
        buck teeth, which mouthwash I rinsed.
                A *Lee Press On Nail* never tastes good coming up.

But oh, how my mama could swing her hips to *Swing Low*
        when her husband left to fly drones
                with his boyfriend.

I knew he wasn't supposed to have one.
        Neither was I.
                But my priest wasn't exactly a boyfriend.

Swing low, sweet chariot, coming for to carry me home.
        My mama spat in my mouth like
                that territorial cardinal

the vermilion who did not know how
        to migrate, the one who bangs her beak against glass
                year after year after year.

Eastern Seaboard

Beneath my sheetless twin bed a shoebox
inside not Mary Janes but a bus schedule and an Eastern Seaboard map
shabby and wavering   Chincoteague frayed
even the palominos couldn't recover
though they taught me to circumvent the rope and teeth click

in the box, rolls of twenties from the heads of nameless men I blew at 16
after riding the waterslide   at the park on days I didn't want to eat
how I learned to save
a granola bar, a change of clothes, a wide-ruled notebook, a pencil,

knew I was deserting my mother   forfeiting the daughter role
but wanted a home   without bedbugs
without bed hands without windchimes beating the frame
a morse code   without hush-hush   without amens
without flying roaches   snared in braces from night walking
night spitting

sometimes sometimes in the morning in this new house
I culled from God's palm   with the sunlight

and the Queen bed   and the deck

in the trees   I remember
to stop   running
to stop   forsaking myself

Sarah, The Fool

As if I could mother myself
As if I could mother myself to mercy
As if I could mother grace offering my own girls
what I did not receive from a half-blind hoarding woman
whose closest friend was the bath that kept her under
and the one who kept her awake: Thomas Jefferson.
The dead never talk back.
The dead won't cease stuttering. I hear their teeth.

As if I could mother myself
As I could mother what I did not hold or have
As if I could make what I could not form
As if I could make what I could not recall
Is not memory the nucleus for shape?

I arrived in full form. Mothered early. Mothered late.
Mothered till half past eight.

As if I could mother myself, I study mothers
how they offer themselves again and again
Even the one named in sacrifice by offering her son Issac
And how she laughs
How I laugh as if I could mother myself—
As if I could wring hands to unhinge rumor from a blindfold
Always Oyster tongued—as if I could mother myself
To let the jellyfish sting, to let all the salt in.

This time

when he comes in
I will
not just roll
over this time, I will not
claw at the wall
will not hold
my breath will not make
myself small this time
I will call out *mama*
your husband is here
did you lose him
and she will stumble
out of her cave with
her one good eye
and stand up
this time, I will
have all my limbs
this time I will be
ready and stab his fat
hairy arm with my lefty scissors
the ones Ms. Underwood gave me
when I finally arrived in third grade
with clean hair and brushed teeth
after the lice fell on my plastic toothbrush;
if I jab these scissors deep enough
in the chamber, it will give
me time to roll off
the bed and slide under it
and out the window
and then he can never
beat me with a T-Square
never take my photo
after his slimy kiss
never demand a root beer float
in a Hardee's glass
and to sit with him to watch
reruns of *M*A*S*H**
this time I will
I will not

look back no matter
how loud he calls me   girl.

How to Smile

By seventeen, I knew to slide open a window without making a sound. Knew the right skirt, right angle to tilt my hip, right corner of Richmond Road to hitchhike on. Knew to avoid the Ford trucks that always stopped and the Camaros that rarely did. I knew the Seven Sacraments, the priest who always preferred me on my knees in his office but upright in the choir loft on Sundays. Knew the Archangel, Michael. Knew the right blond wig to wear in the right hotel to pass as a tourist in a town where everyone is in drag. Knew the back of a movie theatre, how to spend an entire rainy day watching *Shawshank Redemption* for free, and knew it was queer before I knew the word queer. Knew how to blow a stranger long and slow enough for cash for dinner. Because my mama's check from the gas station never lasted. And hunger was familiar. What I didn't know was how to hide cash. How to hide from a stepfather who took pictures of me against any tree on The Colonial Parkway, and then immersed in a chemical developer, rocked my smile shut.

How You Explained Your Mother

There was the morning she parted your teeth with dish soap,
and the morning she lit Marlboros in your twelve-year-old mouth

one after the other, not bothering to flick the ash.
The morning she learned and forgot how her husband

kept you home from school
on the couch, how he never left you in the bath,

the morning her wooden spoon rang your thighs,
the morning she held you over her yellow motorboat

yelling *I am not gonna toss you in, little fuck up,*
the morning she left you asleep at the roller rink

the morning she drove from South Carolina to New York
only stopping for you to pee on the side of the road

And the morning she whined:
I tried and tried a hanger, and still, you grew.

The Blood Moon

Ain't no one looking out for you at ten years old.
I come to you, and you don't know my name.

After thirty-five years,
I have been more loyal than the woman you married

whose hand you saw up an assistant's skirt
more loyal than her ghost, who keeps saying

I am sorry every morning
at your bedside.

More loyal than the priest who claimed you had potential.
More loyal than the nurse who ran at the sight of me.

There were the months I watched when your girls came
and months after divorce, when I grew and grew into a fibroid

lifted your steps back from the nurse who was not the right man for you
made you pass out in front of your girls;

you were pale one night and couldn't tell the EMT
where the blood was coming from.

Couldn't be touched. Couldn't even stand.
He asked if you had been raped, and all you could say was

not this time.

When I was twelve

my brothers made pocket change or more
off my throat.

I wanted to destroy that pinecone fort
where they tied me down

before those mullet boys laughed
my pink lip gloss off their cock-

before they ran their Tuesday train,
betting which one would pin me,

in my blue and white bikini, which said
Voluez-vous coucher avec moi ce soir?

I couldn't speak French at twelve.
My mouth didn't say anything loud enough.

But now, in this City of Angels, cactus, and lizards
and miles and decades from those oak trees—

I begged to fall on my little frame—

I make and remake my breath,
next to my lemon tree
                                        grown and not grown
                                        as that mirror girl in a bikini,

blue and white, checkered with French.

Tie

My brother, who used to let his friends fuck me for money,
drove me to Ithaca from Williamsburg. My mother made him.

We did not speak for hours. He smoked pot the entire way.
I vomited after medium rare burgers at *Bob's Big Boy.*

He had a seizure but did not die, my mother
asked me to pray for him.

How do you pray for a ghost?
If only the gods are willing. They rule the vaulting skies.

There are those who tell me I am to forgive.
I do not want to carry him into every line, every walk in the forest.

I wish him dead. Not well.
I would tie the rope myself.

I bet he would say the same.

You don't know me, but you have been inside me

They painted her vagina blue to check for abrasions.
Swabbed inside her vulva and anus,

they pointed a Nikon between her legs
and then let her shower.

She wanted to take off her body and deposit in the emergency room.
She had been found behind a dumpster.

Necklace tied around her neck.
She read about her assault; learned what happened the way the world did.

Brock said: *if I wanted to know her, I would have asked for her number.*
Brock said: *I didn't plan on taking her back to my dorm.*

Brock said: *I took off her underwear. I touched her.*
But I never actually raped her.

Brock said: *She liked it. I made her come.*

They pulled pine needles out of her hair, tested for HIV,
gave her a sweatshirt. And sent her home.

As a girl, I did not know the back of a dumpster.
Only my twin bed, the flatbed of a truck

in a field, the inside of a frat's bathroom,
the bottom of the bleachers.

I cannot recall the first time I said no,
Only how loud and how often.

Twenty-Six Ways to Take a Photo

Apollo 8 astronauts took a Christmas Eve photo called *Earthrise* from the moon.

Blue hour the holy space before sunrise when the sun submits to the horizon.

Countless beautiful fuckboys request full-body pics from Bumble texts. To break the unspoken rule that curvy girls only post headshots. If I send you my head to toe, do you promise to bend me over, make me moan, take out the trash, always come with flowers and a book? Would you like an image of my occipital lobe or perhaps an entire x-ray of the cauliflower between my ears?

Daguerreotypes require iron and mercury vapor to impose the image on a silver plate. Elements embedded in our earliest reflections. The toxins killed the artists. Whose hands polished all those silver plates before the image came alive?

Eastman in Rochester, New York, is the world's oldest photography museum, with more than 400,000 photographic objects. I am not a museum. But when hysterical, I feel historical.

Frida Kahlo said *I want to be inside your darkest everything.* The photograph is the only route.

Getting makeup and hair done, I hunted pretty like a deer. I thought curling and extensions and lashes would make me forget the eye bags from waking in the night begging God. Thought I could erase twenty years. Beautiful, too far of a stretch to call myself.

How do I look is both transitive and intransitive. How do I see the frame, and how do I appear in it? I am both subject and object. Still, I cannot be curated and hung.

Invisible is how I feel most of the time. A head with beautiful boobs and feet. If I am no longer the object in your frame, will you stop trying to focus on me? If I am only an object in your frame, will you even see me?

Jeremy was the name of the soldier who took me to the Eastman. On his arm, he had tattooed the Seven Dwarfs.

Kahlo posed for the camera, met her audience eye to eye, making herself in her own image. I study her to drink courage.

Learning not to critique crows feet on my eyes or the rolls on my core or the double chin is a practice I have yet to embrace. Nightly, I stand in front of the mirror and tell myself lies.

Men act, and women appear. Men look at women. Women watch themselves being looked at. The surveyor is a woman in herself is male: the surveyed is female. Thus, she turns herself into an object of vision: a sight, says John Berger. I am a sight to be reckoned with. I am not easy to lose. Or forget.

Never mind that I have not been kissed this year around the sun. Men are not the weather. I glow like a motherfucker in photos without one.

Orient the earth from the moon. What would *Earthrise* look like now?

Photoshoot in morning sunlight with a photographer who makes me laugh. She doesn't want to touch me, and I am so relieved.

Quietly I learn to fuck with the lights on. But I am not quiet.

Record the image with light in one moment. Chinese philosophers had the idea for a light box in the fifth century: a photogram: Greek for light drawing. Expose the surface to light.

Seeing comes before words. The child looks and recognizes before it can speak.

The first woman I loved texted after twenty years for photos of our life back in Tokyo. She wants them for a fiftieth birthday party her husband is planning. She is dying of cancer. I sent the pics of us in orange kimonos at Hakone. I am not invited to crabcakes and mimosas in Manhattan. Girlfriends rarely have an act two. We want to remember who we were. Who we are is unimaginable.

Unravel how he drove you to daddy-daughter dates or so he called them—to pull-offs on the Parkway in Virginia. Against an oak whose branches could not protect you, you refused to smile through braces and rubber bands. He would always touch your hair and click the Nikon. In this moment, you left yourself. You are still looking for her.

Valiant to post new photos on the website.

Why do I not have any photos of my mother? Because she spent my childhood working at a gas station and nearly drowning herself. Now I see how water calls all of us by name.

X-rays of my fibroid, the size of a cauliflower, hung in the window so I would not forget how I passed out in front of my daughters.

Yet to oblige my trainer who wants me to track weekly photos. What could change in a week? Never been into the before and after. I took one photo six weeks in to see if my body would actually change. Was pretty a state I could arrive in? Inches have fallen off; pounds not as quick to go. The weight I need to lose is not on my body.

Zeitgeist of my face: fragile like a bomb and an orchid.

Ars Poetica

This pink moon, a misnomer;
Indigenous people call it a frog moon,

the growing moon, the egg moon,
the moon when the ducks come back.

It's more of a golden hue, named
after- for- the creeping phlox-

a pink wildflower, a star shape, first to bloom.
On the first of the month, I draw Justice

in her right hand, a sword- I have missed this-
been busy looking at the scales she holds,

knowing gravity's burden, wanting balance
chasing harmony, weighing feathers against hearts,

for the Libra in my chart to harmonize my flames,
for a Libra to flame, singular my glance of late

(has been one hundred and twenty-one days
since another's hand-- a heart--a weight.)

I lay on the frozen ground for Spring
as if he were a lover who blocked me,

who does not like the way I call his name,
whispering to the crocus who have burst through an inch.

Putting my ear to the earth to listen hard.
Soul and soil are only a vowel apart.

Perhaps this right side of Justice I must see.
Between two pillars, forced to pay my debt

every sword I have swallowed to keep
relationships intact has severed my glottis.

I draw out each blade by blade by blade by blade.
Wasting not one wound, not one sorrow till my tongue is free.

II. Lucky to Keep You

"Half alive to the brightening sky, half dead already."

Ada Limon

A Lucky Find

A red fox ran by my window with a fawn's head
in his mouth. Eye to eye with decapitated fawn,
I was thirsty to trap head in teeth,
If I could be that lucky, luck is coming and going,
I scoured for a deer carcass
expected to see a mourning mama or an orange
bandana wet with chew, a bullet, expected
the flies to usher me back home, to reap the dead
where they belong but find instead
the deer who can smell fox on me, fox in me,
fox before me. Everyone can; I have severed my head
for every fox who called me beautiful
craved to be ruby with head in jaw
to be crimson and free.

The Substitute Boyfriend or Why I am not a Side Dish (a found poem)

I.
Tomato flowers are not the only part of the plant that responds to vibration.
It has been twelve months since

Researchers played loud sounds in a high C, and ripening ceased for six days.
I have felt you pull my hair.

Vibrations impact the way fruit manufactures hormones.
Or anyone for that matter.

Cheerful yellow tomato flowers are shaped like a wizard's hat.
I might forget how.

They need to be shaken to release their pollen.
When you said I should by now, know to change my voice to sound like your friend, because she was there, I wanted gazpacho and your head.

The Aztecs called them a plump thing with a naval.
I was never too fat for you.

Lycopene is an antioxidant that protects human cells from damage.
And I fit easily in your mouth.

They are cousins of a belladonna plant and once used to kill wolves.
I bet she doesn't fit as well.

They were once considered an aphrodisiac.
I bet she never talks back.

Heirloom varieties are open-pollinated.
You made me hate my own—

II.
Licorice is a chest-high, bushy shrub. But it flowers.
I thought you did not play games.

Glycyrrhizin is 50 times sweeter than sucrose, and it causes high blood pressure.
The first time you hurt me, I laughed it off.

In Chinese medicine, it balances gland function. The Greek spelling Glykoriza means sweet root. Sweet rot?

Every other laugh was pretending.

Eating five grams or more daily of licorice can cause heart arrhythmia and muscle weakness.

How long was she around before you announced her?

An arrhythmia is a disturbance in the rhythm of the heartbeat, whether it's too fast or skipping beats. This can be caused by problems with the electrical system. They say Takotsubo syndrome is only temporary and causes rapid but reversible heart muscle weakness, mimicking a heart attack.

Like you, they were lying. Does my name ever cross your tongue?

Here You Are At Rejection Again

Home
sweet home. Doorbell knows your finger.
Larger Self says
its redirection. Says he's an idiot.
I mean, really. Have you seen this profile?
I mean   damn.
The resilience alone sparkles.
But the Other You unveiled
everything, more than all the others.
Still, he said no,
thank you. Always only fuckable.
Friendable.
You thought vulnerability the path.
You are beginning to see it as a liar.

Do not make a man tell you more than once
he does not want you,
though he professes feelings and desire,
he does not want you,
put on the breaks he said,
though he appreciates you, values you,
likes the connection, he does not want you.
Stop reaching.   Just stop.

Fold up your heart, spleen, and throat,
crease like the crane you are, and know how to be
and run. He is not the weather.
Not the sky.

Tell yourself you are not an idiot for loving him,
for believing yourself loveable for believing him.
Tell yourself you are gorgeous and whole before
and after him.   Tell yourself he will miss you.
He will look for you   in all others to come.
Not one will know how to bind vowel
against consonant, not one will ever be in your galaxy.

When the animals

still talk to you after he left town
and you are not yet a fish murderer

stop turning around, thinking he will call you woman.
You wring hands and bills and remember

How he always called you gold.
Fluorescent lights blind, and hamsters' spin

You miss him the damn green dragon spits.

Your body parts won't come back. Nor will his.

You haven't let go, says the tortoise.

You don't know how.

He won't speak, says the snake.

His tongue and heart no longer yours.

They never were.

Temporary

When you reached out to see if I was alive
if the girls were healthy
I thought I have not forgotten
how I was late you were late

Have not forgotten the other women
I had to share you with
Have not forgotten the hours you polished your Mercedes
but not the empty fish tanks
or the dusty piano you never played
The three pairs of Italian leather shoes lined by the door.
Your TV in the bathroom
Just above the hot tub
how you stood me up
your hands pulled on my nipples
and your mouth took me

Have not forgotten the scrubs I starched and ironed
Your white shirts, the cashmere cardigan I borrowed,
the broken bed, the toys
no evidence, no trace
have not forgotten how I had to leave three times
before I was finally gone

because your mama's kitchen in Queens kept me
Kahlo exhibit in the gardens kept me
when you held my friend's newborn and pulled
me into frame
I could almost see you as husband

and I believed
until the others rang, and you answered
in the car, in the restaurant, in the bar
even with you, it was never just you
and I was just short of casual,
temporary, convenient, optional
until I was not

Thirteen Reasons I Am More Than a Good Idea for the Man Who Said I was not

Because I am an amazing expert
Because I could have been your unicorn
Because I have thesaurus lips and a gospel heart
Because I take dictation and give it to
Because I love your dog's print on my white sweater
Because I am more than a snow globe with an ocean
Because I am more than a timeshare in the Dominican
Because I got men who still recite how I shed for them
Because I offered more than an apple
Because my ass isn't bad, and there are so many initials after my name
Because I call the sentence home
Because nothing neat is fun, and nothing dry is either
Because I am the city where the tongue gym thrives.

But You Were Not Cold

You told me every woman before
saw you as a walk-in freezer
that I was not to drop by
to wait for an invitation even before knocking
even if close to not touch
anything without permission
to let go of needs
to focus on what matters
the spinach, the salmon
but not you
you said we should stop
because the end would be worse
I couldn't fathom an end
I would have carried your books
though you were six five and 290 pounds
and didn't need me to carry anything
I would have walked your pit bulls
would have opened up the sentence
and gagged my own hum

The Panther

You were quick to let me walk away from that store
and in the fluorescent Big Box, you said
I feel you, you said, *Woman*
woman before handing me a filter
I see you I see you
though you are long gone
from this mall, this town, this state.
Your panther frame there and not there
my declaration only an echo—

at home in the tank you gave me, I clean,
curse you and the two fat goldfish
swimming away from each other
you were here to remind me I could
love
love never evaporates, my dear panther,
it only quiets, humming,
like the tank light, the stones,
so for the love of God
how did I end up here
again—

Casting

You common nightcrawler.
I still swing you from city to city.
Call your name asleep. I miss

the soft baits, the lure, the hooked worm.
How temperate you were with my girl.
At the park, she squished worm

between forefinger and thumb,
held it up and split its head on the hook.
She loved dead things.

You wanted her to thread the worm
on the shaft of the hook.
She caught a silver sunfish whose body flapped

but tossed him back because she felt sorry.
You told me if I kept flapping,
you would go quiet.

I thought, not me. I met your mother,
the one no girl met till it mattered.
On the same table where you kissed me,

you served red snapper.
You licked fish bones and all.
Wanted me to crunch bones.

But my tender tongue resisted.
I listened over and over to your bait preparation:
How my dress was never short enough.

My scales never shiny enough.
I had too many initials after my name.
How I refused to come up for air.

Mimicry

Dead cardinals slap the sidewalk like a rug.
(Will I die in New York?)

Red half-wings greet me under foot.
Step over broken beaks.
(Did they all give up mid-flight?)

I want to believe it is not a metaphor for my half a century.
Not a blackbird to see thirteen times.

Not a woodpecker to hide from.
Not a bluejay who brings messages of wealth—

(What beak of myself did I return to find?)

I pin God like a monarch or a viceroy to a board.
Nabokov would be jealous.
(How long will Cayuga Lake call me to the bottom?)

Who is more toxic: the lake, the butterfly, or the pin?
The viceroy mimics the monarch.
(Which am I?)

Fort recall where I thought brothers would protect
and not pin me on a board, but they ran a train
(Is this the last train?)

I thought a man could fuck the grief out of me.
Why did I think any man could?
(I nearly died in mimicry.)

Not a Homemaker

I don't live
in your heart.
Though you say, I could
squat there.
I want to believe
you won't auction it out
to the highest bidder.
          Who are you when
you have not seen me
in weeks, and you have me
in between your legs
and welcome home
is the first word out
of your mouth.
          I am not your homemaker,
Not a housewife, a lover
of brick and mortar.
          I would rather spit-shine
my dream of runways and oceans
of bioluminescence
of the island of Maldives
where the stars come
and submit to the undertow.

The Rhythm

I do not know why you cover my face when
you are inside of me I reach
for your sharp jawline with my hands—
I   say   look   at   me

You are bone after bone—hollow, a reed,
a recorder when you are supposed to be open
you disappear—disconnect from the bind,

from your taut skin on my couch.
I could have whistled through your skeleton
who had lost all in Hurricane Maria.

I could have been any other curvy mama
who wanted to be seen but settled for invisibility.
I do not heed the warning, the siren,

the rise of the tide. I turn off the channel.
Ignore the wind chimes.
I talk myself out of myself

on the regular—
I allow you to cross me
Sometimes I break

my own self before you
get the chance; I dare you;
I'll beat you to it.

Lease

When an object reverses
direction
its instantaneous velocity
is zero.
Distance and time
are ghosts of estrangement.
Longing never ceases,
nor does reason.

How can I take up residency
in another
when I have only known
how to squat?
I have never been an owner,
always on lease.
How can I place a sign
that says welcome home
when I have never thought
I was sovereign,
a structure worth bending.

I move to the space of other
another, any other,
evacuate, then lap in
and out of another sack of flesh
with irrelevant names.
Begging the other to do the work.

What would it mean to not leave
to cease lapping the nameless?
Would grace come?
Would I recognize her?
Would she know my name?

Go No Contact

I don't want to know if you miss me,
if there is another woman in your kitchen, I am sure there is,
grateful, as I was to be there, even as an understudy,
knew I was an understudy, thought
I could love you to the lead, or cut off my own hand
to do so, you always preferred me slightly injured,
a little bit smaller, I did not leave the first time
of the betrayal, so I allowed it, turned
my head from it, lying to myself about denial.

How you recalibrated me
so I could not compound the events
always a new beginning
cycle of slap, apology, gift, repeat.
You told me to be quiet, or not so proud of myself.
I never wanted to be big around you,
never chose expansion, always on a dimmer,
hands on the wall, ass in air, the kind of invitation
you never had to RSVP to.
Conditioned as I was to your command.
I cut my own sentences in half.
The gift after the shove does not erase the shove.
The gift after the shove does not erase the shove.

How to Leave a Man

Let me exhale him
so I don't keep wishing

he would call me baby
Let me take a machete

through dense underbrush
a sharp one-sided blade used for cane

Let it be a truck hydroplaning
on the exit spinning in the guard rail

Let brights fail so the end can't be witnessed
Let the driver be asleep and not on the phone

Let the crossover be a blink
the gate still open

Let the watches start working again
Let me get up from this table

Anything but this braided rope
where the constant twist withers me

how it burns my palm as it unravels
how the tree branch echoes the river delta

how the fractal claims my eye
Let it be lightning that scissors the sky

In The End

all forms are lost, the energy of our gesture splinters.
I palm the book of Basho, trace Kanji on rice paper
wait on the bullet train that turns cherry blossoms into winter.

I no longer dream in gold. Can't offer you any more hints.
You can't even find the station while I pan through a river
for form. You have lost the energy for a gesture. Splinters

between us are half specter and half prophesy. Rent
the possibility of violin strings: will you shiver?
Wait, how my train turns your blossom to winter,

dark the morning hostess, dark the mezzotint
of ink on our copper hearts stuffed with dried feathers.
All forms lost. The energy of our gesture splinters

towards the probability of bones, but vows and a hint
of quince and ginger jam, swimming in pool together
unimaginable. My train will turn cherry blossoms into winter,

grind buds to snow, skeletons to ash.
Why remain with you to season, to remember?
Form has lost her energy. Your gesture splinters
and my bullet train turns our blossoms into winter.

After You Left Town

I learn that time is warped
to stop thinking crumbs meant
there was or would be bread
to stop chasing what burns
to spoon vows in my own voice

in the morning I pluck the dead
from my bloodstream
one hollow quill at a time
sometimes I call it prayer
other days I call it execution

No one after

you has checked the windows from the inside
to see if they are locked no one
after you has asked if I have eaten
no one after you has reminded me to take
the potatoes out of the oven
no one after you has reminded me to put the stamp
on the corner of the bill
no one after you has pulled on my nipples the same
no one after you has pulled
no one after you has called me gold
                                    but the gods, some say, have a way
                                                                        of sucking out all the gold

Keys

Branches know my name.
I sit on a slanted rooftop
with a bottle
of Jack and a notebook
fingering the bag of motel keys
Pine trees begging me—
so I return to rooms
at the Red Roof Inn
that were once bought
for me
by a priest
who was running
from God
and the ghost of his dead child.
I have not yet traded Jack for tea.
Resistant to time
my sense seeped out of my fishbowl.
She got sick of rattling my skull.

III. Lucky to Lose You

You will love again the stranger who was your self.
Give wine. Give bread. Give back your heart
to itself, to the stranger who has loved you

all your life, whom you ignored
for another, who knows you by heart.
Take down the love letters from the bookshelf,

the photographs, the desperate notes,
peel your own image from the mirror.
Sit. Feast on your life.

Derek Walcott

Dear Sonia

in meditation you arrive
still platinum blonde, red lips
and fake fur with a shiny broach

Your black shirt says other
Your frozen chihuahua
and Pasadena succulents spin around your feet

I taste the soba we ate in Cali and Tokyo
smell cloves in your fingers
Do you smoke in heaven

Have the tumors gone above or below
Do you tell Jesus what to do
Since you left me for him

Jesus, the lucky one

You tell me to stay on the mat

when the bridge
would mean I could see you
I want to see you

You see me

On the anniversary of your death
I wonder why you would never hold my hand in public
Never say we were more than friends

Never say we were—
You would hate this poem
How I placed you here

Other poems made you stop talking
I am sorry for holding you
in the bedroom and not the dance floor

Sorry, I did not want
to be your secret
Sorry the pulpit was the place you loved more—

I am calling all of it
disaster on the anniversary
of your death, I remember

the job interview I failed in Montclair
the school I wanted to belong to
how lost I felt

how lost
how lost
a block from the funeral

I was not welcome at Princeton or the church
your husband with his own priestly collar
took one look at my red hair and slammed the door

the stoop I sat on
flask in hand
waiting for you to finally say

Sarah

On Ithaca

What exactly did Odysseus return to?
What story is not a ghost story?

Let me try again. I came here after Tokyo.
Could not believe I had landed Cornell.

I was married for ten years. She only touched me in the first.
Preferred the bottle or any other woman who did not ask her to put it down.

I could tell you all the names of every other woman she touched
instead but the line is not long enough, and this town is small.

Each and every one had flour in her hair.
It was my own kind of war where I put down the pencil.

When Odysseus had returned, his dog and nurse recognized him
but no one else did. I could not recognize myself.

One who gave up poems for pastries. What could I possibly say?
I want a dog, but do not have one. Had a nurse, but I left

because he had another woman. *In the cursed kingdom, each summer, they hang*
twelve maidens. I tied the rope myself. More than once.

I have long stopped being a maiden. This is supposed to be home.
Let me try again.

The Year

There was the year you promised to quit smoking and the year you did not.

The year you promised no more debt over lamb and green beans.

The year sugar blinded me, and you made bunnies out of chocolate.

The year you made me write investors, knock on the bank's door.

The year we stood in front of the Patisserie sign with my name on it.

The year I finally published a book.

The year you begged me to throw away the pencils.

The year I begged you for a baby.

The year I begged you for another.

The year I resolved not to beg.

The year I resolved not to.

The year I resolved.

So much of any year is flammable.

So much of a marriage will burn.

Just Married

Honor   the yoke honor the oxen   the ass
married twice   first time not actually legal
a hundred guests a white dress a fancy house under construction
chicken and asparagus and your marzipan cake
The second   a waterfall
You were two hours late   making cake
I excused this   you didn't say any vows
before we turned arm and arm
you looked through me and said: *Let's get this over with*
I excused this   you were shy
you avoided me at the picnic reception
though you were watching our children
hula in wigs and tutus
Drove myself home in a wedding dress you stumbled
I'm tired of pretending I want to be married.
I excused this
let you stay   because I vowed
your name would be the last word out of my mouth
before I exhaled   because I was drunk on sugar
you came home drunk   on our balcony smoked Marlboros
for hours   a shell   you stopped coming home
I excused this

Even as your new bony girl made a movie
Without your face   just rows and rows of hands
you enrobing chocolate to pop music   a ghost in the machine

When you moved out   you would not take clothes
When it became clear you would not return
I left them at the Patisserie that bore my name

Came home to find all pots missing and my Olivetti.
You don't even write. Pictures turned my face cut out of the frame
Sold the ring the dress the tables
After mediation you whisper over the parking meter:
the ending is all your fault shut the fuck up and play nice
I excused this

But I woke to a day I decided not to slit my own wrist
And You
You were always that hardware store where I kept looking for oranges

After Marriage

You tell me you need to stand your ground.
As if I made it solid.

As if you step on the line, all backs will break.
I am learning to jump over your entrance.

No time for greetings, prologues, salutations.
No longer interested in what you are expecting.

You only speak on the page
and then you have the new one do it as if she was you.

She will never write for you as well as I did.
She is a seamstress.

And I, a banshee who howls at the sight of your lies.
I have evicted my own spine.

How willing I was to be in your made-up world.
How willing I was to be it.

Learning to Speak After Divorce

I am training my tongue to drive. It is slow to learn.
Tongue not brief. The floor of my mouth does not have a margin
for error. Does not have a sign for break.

Tongue cannot swing properly inside my lips
to produce sound. Or even a clear note.
I am sticky and mistuned—mis-tongued.

I cannot fit together in a groove. I cannot even capture
the half-beautiful or half-ugly winged male prey
who lay themselves down for me.

Tongue the garden, Tongue the tree called life
as my exile is the only tune towards home.

New Year's Ash

These first few days of the New Year
I want to toss on my boots and zip
up my windbreaker and begin the ascent

over the hill and grass between the two willows.
I would do this for you even though I hate nature
and I like my nails; I want to yank the grass up,
dig and dig. I am tired of being brave.

I want to stand together in the grave because even when
we were married you ran from me.
I want to stomp your casket
Bootprint your fat face
and beat the living shit out of your skeleton.
Can one beat a skull?
Pummel ash?

And I want to spit on your last few bones in my hand
for leaving me with two girls
for leaving two girls without ever apologizing.

And holding what is left of you
in my left hand I would whisper
thank you, thank you, thank you.

Hook

What I keep tugging out of my scapula
How I swear you pull from the other world
How deep the metal lives in my epidermis
How you blind with every blink of light
every dead cat
and on our anniversary in the gazebo
where we took the girls to feed the carp
I felt your yellow Marlboro-stained fingers twisting
the silver eye deeper
my deltoid resisting your tug
why do you touch me more now since you are dead
than in those years we were married
I would have given a lung
for one of your palms
in mine
dead you can finally be faithful

Wild Turkey

It is true what you heard. I buried a woman I had played wife to but forgot my lines, and her girlfriend, my skinny understudy stepped in; even our children loved the way she never lifted her eyes. The first problem was that I lifted mine. The second that I connected sky to earth and understood sky on the inside. I was the tree who held out the last branch of leaves till the New Year. A winter resistor. It is true. There was a pine box. A wife in it. Children who tossed in dirt. I didn't want them to, but the shovel wouldn't touch me. A wild turkey witnessed from the oak. The younger understudy, with her eyes on the dirt, recited love. I was mute as a monk still reading the pistachio cakes the wife made twelve years before. Understudy toasted the wife, tossed shot glasses in. No one said a liver floats a heart. Or a hand that says I do but never did. Vowless. The first problem was that I lifted my eyes. The second that I drew sky to earth. My youngest dropped in irises, dressing the pine box. Others tossed in anniversary coins, even limes and umbrellas. Because the dead are always thirsty.

First Anniversary

Even in the ground I am not sure it is you.
Frida seems to know exactly where you lie.
I forgot bug spray. A windbreaker.

But not the irises.
I didn't want but Frida did—
Spring wind and cow dung.

A peacock saunters by spreads his blue feathers.
Two mangy dogs sit near the oak tree.
I swat a mosquito and then another.

Even the grass will not grow over you.
Frida asks for a moment and then drops the irises,
and how cruel it was not to let the wine go.

How cruel to choose a bottle over her.
And I wish you alive just to hear this
from a child and then I don't.

And let it be forty years before
she holds my ashes in her hand.

Thirteen

Not surprised my thirteen-year-old child
cannot hold a book
in the year the other mother
drank herself down under

I stopped reading, speaking, eating, at thirteen
before that, libraries were my home base
libraries my pitch my mound

thirteen the year I laid
eyes on my ghostly father for the first and last time

thirteen the year I survived a cock
in a pickup truck who praised God
and tobacco stained my throat

thirteen the year I chased vodka and aspirin
as if they were saints
who could fuck me clean

On Looking

Sometimes in the face of Frida I see Frida
sometimes in the face of Frida I see my ten-year-old self
wanting someone to notice why I am wailing
why I can't stop pissing the bed wanting someone
to notice the blood to notice
my teeth, yellow with
not being able to say: Help
in the face of Frida I see my mama and I don't want to
look sometimes in the face of Frida I see
my mama who loves Jeopardy and the pages
of a history book and a cup of peppermint tea
who loves balsamic and mushrooms and embroidery
sometimes in the face of Frida I see my mama's ten-year old self
in the face of Frida I see Frida sometimes
in the face of Frida I see the Divine
every time
in the face of Frida I see

How I Lie to My Daughters

My girls take turns waking me in the night
because they dream, I fell down an elevator shaft
and they couldn't reach my hand

or that some student shot me in class
because he did not like the grade I gave him.
They wake me at 2 and, 3 and 4 to say

I blew up in the plane or the bus
or the car or the train
in their dream, and they kept calling out.

Every night, I pull them into bed with me,
lay their hand on my stomach and say
Feel it. It is my breath. I ain't dying. Not today.

And we oblige this lie night after night,
that death will pass over
because she only takes one mother at a time.

Prayer

I want to prick your finger
and measure your blood to know what it needs

In case the virus touches you
to see what is missing in your blood

So that I can vitamin it in
Or cook it in or read it in
One measure at a time

How much I want to protect
how worry is a thief of rest
a down payment for a purchase I do not want to buy

So, I call in antibodies and swimming pools
masks and gloves
a chai latte and an angel

I call in back decks and recitals
graduations and weddings
salmon and Bok choy and wasabi pistachios

a black lab and libraries
book launches and reviews
and all of the oceans

and mostly the one to hold my hand on a bench
beneath cherry blossoms for all the rest of my breaths

California Fog

The cloud the curtain—
sight itself a useless privilege:

learn to listen for the approaching car
wet tires

my teenage daughter's disgruntled breath,
her own leg back in Ithaca, her other in this city

of chances, neither foot on the pedal.
Leo's full moon a dress rehearsal.

My value no longer in what I do
or how I lay down to mother

either or both—
the one I slipped out of,

or the one who slipped out of me.

On Your Birthday

resurrection is your middle name. You make the phoenix jealous. Daily, you whip obedience from the ashes. You know how to set fire when they all swore it was out for the night and had doused the pit with spring water. You were not to make it this far. The fallen one who held you in the fort, held you at the altar, halved and quartered you, strung you across kindling, seasoned and turned you as if you were swine, called you suie and spit, the fallen who one fried you in a pot of oil to close to the garage, all have evaporated. Here you are, surprised at 48 in a green chair, with a jade and a window, begging the clock to breathe a little longer (go further) begging the virus to keep her lips off you, though you haven't been kissed this year. Forgetting the tongue of another in your mouth. Still, you buy lipstick. Still, you floss. Hope is the thing with feathers. And your father arrived this year for the second act you might have, and you want to take his hand, say my lines are yours, and look at our thumbs, but you still wonder how long he will stay. He wasn't here in the first half of your life. But now is what is. You are Source, and you are in no hurry to meet Source, though you are thinking of making a death folder for the children. As if a binder with color coded files could mother them. You teach them to set fire and to be the water. You know they will live without you. You are betting on it.

The Pool, the Frog, and the Sound of Water

A long river running
love is
fishes eyes fill with tears
earth shakes just enough to remind us
sound of water the frog the pool
the present tense a lost syllable
if the eye is the haiku of the sun does God
wish for the moon
what has not been
seen
what is not
seen
eyes harvest regret
God a word a tremor
waiting for an idea
a light an edge
lonely echo a light
a beginning wave
in the vibration
Eden was already Eden
when the gardener arrived
who then did God speak
to before Adam—

My East Coast Taurus

I.
For the bulb
for the seed buried in the cup on the school window
for my little bull teacher,
I sleep under the tree with grass blankets
sleep in a fun house

foundations are not yet pine box mirrors to sleep in
little boxes with door frames
even those do not yet feel like coffins

share distress   proclaim water

                                        when I go who will pour into her

share water   proclaim distress

May girl wants trees who have driven
driven trees who know the sky won't break branches
all the other trees who dress like her   make her laugh
all the other trees on the block who listen
a root   a stump with rings
my little May girl pines for a permeant address

II.
She grows weary
of her airport catch-up Honey Crisp mama
          who lost her owl, her pigeon

weary of her half-centaur mama
                    the hoarse throat wail weary
always gallop ready   always at the edge of the paddock

aint no barn doors here strong enough
aint no hay

perhaps if I could lose that horse she would listen
perhaps if I show her
how to mother when mother has no tree or root or seed

III.
My May girl prefers viola strings, prefers black ice and hail
prefers trees who hear the blushing hour
who spell auburn shades that make God jealous or evident
anything but this bamboo or palm or cacti
in the West Coast yard I rent
where succulents shiver on my neck

child prefers a soil introspection, a mud flat
                                        to the bridge between veils
when the dead address
when the dead call back the address
the stamp   the little box with door frames
oak by oak   chestnut by chestnut
no more palm by palm

War up I said
Oar up I said.

When the floods come who will be left to row us home
With all the trees we turn our eyes away from
With all the trees we carry

What If?

What if this is a love-in and not a lockdown?
What if the restlessness is a teacher on how to rest?

What if fear and faith are the same thing--
belief in the unseen?

What if the unseen is the good place?
What if the seen is not?

What if place is only five letters
and not a bucket of self-worth?

What if I didn't have to build and build and build
and rebuild home, but could finally find one within?

What if nervousness becomes a lighter nerve?

What if love is the only answer?

Epilogue

Rise

Frida tells me her head is the king
and her heart is the queen
        she wishes her heart would submit
        but sometimes the queen just won't play.

I tell her the heart knows.
        But the brain can order
        the heart to behave.

My heart tantrums, breaks teapots on fishbone wallpaper
        again and again. Blood wills me to not call him
        back because he likes his women voiceless
        and my voices are honeyed.

I have long lost interest in catching boys, bees, or flies.
I am not interested in netting fish.
                But maybe in fishnets and new ink

that reads
        when I fell
                I lost my spark—but when I rise

I rise as the entire flame.

Notes for Lucky to Have YOU

I. Lucky to Find You

Everyone in me is a bird.
I am beating all my wings.
They wanted to cut you out
But they will not.
They said you were immeasurably empty
But you are not.
They said you were sick unto dying.
But they were wrong.
You are singing like a schoolgirl.
You are not torn.
Anne Sexton, "In Celebration of My Uterus"

"The Lime Green Chairs"

This poem includes a reference to *The Book of Common Prayer* which is a liturgical texts of prayers commonly used in the Episcopal and Anglican Church.

"What Father Michael Gave Me"

References Bruton Parish Episcopal Church in Colonial Williamsburg, Virginia.

Let me not to the marriage of true minds admit impediments
*Love is not love which alters when it alteration finds. (*Shakespeare, "Sonnet 116"*)*

Lay your sleeping head, my love
Human on my faithless arm.
Time and fevers burn away
*Individual Beauty from. (*Auden, "Lullaby"*)*

"My Mother's Second Husband"

Swing Low Sweet Chariot, coming for to carry me home are lyrics from an African American Spiritual.

"This Time"

References *M*A*S*H** an 1980s TV show about a medic community during the Korean War.

"How To Smile"

References the movie *Shawshank Redemption*, a 1994 drama based on a Stephen King novel. The Archangel Michael is the leader of the heavenly host and the chief of God's armies. The Seven Sacraments include Baptism, Confirmation, Eucharist, Reconciliation, Anointing of the Sick, Marriage, and Holy Orders.

"When I was Twelve"

The phrase "Voulez-vous coucher avec moi ce soir" translates to "Do you want to sleep with me?

"Tie"

If only the Gods are willing/They rule vaulted skies. It is from *The Odyssey* book 5 (Robert Fagel translation)

"You Don't Know Me"

This is a found poem upon reading Chanel Mille's rape case *People vs. Turner.*

"Twenty-Six Ways"

Earthrise is a photo of Earth taken from orbit in 1968 during the Apollo 8 Mission.

The Eastman Museum in Rochester is the world's oldest photography museum.

Frida Kathlo said: "I want to be inside your darkest everything." In *The Diary of Frida Kahlo: An Intimate Self-Portrait.*

John Berger wrote *Ways of Seeing*, and this text influenced this poem about how Men act, and women appear.

II. Lucky to Keep You

Half alive to the brightening sky, half dead already.
Ada Limon "Salvage"

"The Substitute Boyfriend" borrows found language from posts about planting tomatoes and licorice and Takotsubo syndrome.

"Go No Contact:" The phrase Slap, apology gift repeat is borrowed/ revised from an IG post of Dr. Rhea.

III.

You will love again the stranger who was your self.
Give wine. Give bread. Give back your heart
to itself, to the stranger who has loved you

all your life, whom you ignored
for another, who knows you by heart.
"Love After Love" by Derek Walcott

"On Ithaca"

In the caged kingdom, each summer they hang twelve maidens is revised from "Lies We Sing to the Sea" by Sarah Underwood.

Acknowledgments

"This Time," and "What Father Michael gave me," *Survival & Beyond* by the Survivor Anthology Project at Safe Passage, Summer 2025

"On Your Birthday," *Door is a Jar,* Summer 2025

"A Frog, The Pool," *Croak*, Winter 2025

"No One After," "The Other Mother." "Hook," "A Lucky Find," "The Year," "The Moon," "After Marriage," "Wild Turkey," "First Anniversary," *Eunoia Review*, Feb 2024

"Homemaker," "The Rhythm," *2nd River Review,* December 2024

"A Bamboo Anchor" (renamed to My East Coast Taurus), *Poets for Scientists*, December 2024.

"Eastern Seaboard," *Passengers*, June 2023

"Lease," "Stopbath" (renamed to How to Smile), *On the Seawall*, August 2022

"After You Left Town," *Yuzu Press*, Oct 2022

"Walking to Church," *NY Quarterly,* Fall 2022

"In The End," *Wild Roof Journal*, Jan 2022

"How I Lie to My Daughters," *Cimarron Review*, Winter 2020

"When the Animals," *North American Review*, 2020

"Learning to Speak," "New Year's Ash," *South Florida Poetry Journal*, May 2019

Special thanks to Heather Batelic, Stephanie Cowling-Rich, Toshun Campbell, and Brian Harper, for helping me believe that my gift was meant to be shared and that my story didn't belong to me.

Thanks to Theta Pavis, Maria Bradfield, Danny Bellinger, Alex N. Miller, Dr. Theri Pickens, Mary Gilliland, Dr. Anne Whitney, Rebecca Faulkner, Nikki Newfeld, Dr. Laura Zacharin, and Susan J. Cronin for reading and editing earlier poems in this manuscript.

Special thanks to the Saltonstall Foundation and Community Valley of Writers for their support and resources.

Dr. Sarah Jefferis holds a BA and an MA from Hollins University, an MFA in Poetry from Cornell, and a PhD in Lit and Creative Writing from Binghamton University. Poetry publications include *Forgetting the Salt* (Foothills Press, 2008) and *What Enters the Mouth* (Standing Stone Books, 2017), as well as poems/essays that have appeared in *The North American Review, The Catamaran, The Cimarron Review, Rhino, The American Literary Review, The Patterson Review, Door is a Jar, NYQ, Croak, On the Seawall, The Wild Roof Journal* and others. She has been a poetry and essay fellow at the Saltonstall Foundation of the Arts in New York, The Community of Writers in California, and MASS MoCA in Massachusetts. She has completed her first novel, entitled *Running After Jesus,* as well as a lyrical essay collection about the blessings and difficulties of single motherhood. Her most important calling is to raise two powerful feminist children who love themselves and who are willing to speak out against racial and economic injustice. She is currently working on creating her first play about growing up in Colonial Williamsburg, Virginia, and the systemic problems of abuse in the Episcopal Church.

In addition to being a Senior Lecturer at Cornell, she is also the CEO of her own writing consultant business called Write. Now. whose mission includes using yoga to help clients move through writing blocks. She is a certified Yoga teacher through Mighty Yoga, where she currently teaches Yin yoga. She is the founder of *Mat to Pen*, a yoga writing workshop that designs reflective journal writing prompts to help clients move from post-traumatic stress to post-traumatic growth.

Moreover, Dr. Jefferis serves as an intuitive writing coach for creative leaders who need editorial assistance at any stage of their writing project. She designs writing workshops to explore issues of equity and inclusion, as well as generative workshops in poetry and non-fiction. Additionally, she offers poetry readings and keynotes on using writing as a healing modality for trauma survivors. Her most recent TEDX is entitled: “Writing a Prescription for Healing” and can be found at https://www.youtube.com/watch?v=S3lkSvI5rUQ
You can find her at www.sarahjefferis.com.

www.ingramcontent.com/pod-product-compliance
Lightning Source LLC
LaVergne TN
LVHW090535110826
845146LV00003B/1103

* 9 7 9 8 8 9 9 9 0 4 8 2 0 *